LEX ORANDI, LEX CREDENDI:

LITURGY, DOCTRINE AND SCRIPTURE IN HISTORY AND TODAY

MARTIN DAVIE

The Latimer Trust

ISBN 978-1-906327-54-5

Cover photo: "Hands folded in prayer on a Holy Bible in church concept for faith, spirituality and religion" from rahwik

Published by the Latimer Trust January 2019.

The Latimer Trust (formerly Latimer House, Oxford) is a conservative Evangelical research organisation within the Church of England, whose main aim is to promote the history and theology of Anglicanism as understood by those in the Reformed tradition. Interested readers are welcome to consult its website for further details of its many activities.

The Latimer Trust

London N14 4PS UK

Registered Charity: 1084337

Company Number: 4104465

Web: www.latimertrust.org

E-mail: administrator@latimertrust.org

Latin phrases and their meanings

There are a series of Latin phrases that are widely used in theology such as *sola scriptura, sola fide* and *ecclesia reformata semper reformanda*. One thing they all have in common, apart from saying things that are theologically significant, is that their meaning needs careful unpacking if it is to be understood properly.

Thus, the phrase *sola scriptura* ('Scripture alone') does not mean that the Bible is the only rule of Christian faith and practice in the sense that no Christian should either believe anything or do anything that is not explicitly mandated in the Bible. As Richard Hooker points out in the *Laws of Ecclesiastical Polity*, this is an extreme position which is it is impossible to live out in consistently in everyday life. 'For in every action of common life to find out some sentence clearly and infallibly setting before our eyes what we ought to do, (seem we in Scripture never so expert,) would trouble us more than we aware.'[1] Try deciding between a flat white and a latte in your local coffee shop on the basis of an explicit sentence in Scripture on the issue and you will see what Hooker is getting at.

What the phrase *sola scriptura* does mean is that Scripture is the supreme authority in all matters of doctrine and practice. There are other authorities, such as Christian tradition and the exercise of sanctified reason, that the individual Christian and the Church collectively may rightly draw on to shape what they think and what they do, but all such other authorities are subordinate to, and subject to correction by, the written word of God.

In similar fashion, the phrase *sola fide* ('by faith alone') does not mean that there is no need for the Christian to exercise the virtues of hope and love (1 Corinthians 13:13) or for the Christian to perform good works (James 2:14–17). What it does mean is that the way a Christian enters into,

---

[1] Richard Hooker, *The Laws of Ecclesiastical Polity*, Bk.II.viii.6, (Oxford: OUP, 1841), p.273.

and remains in, a right relationship with God is through faith in the saving work of God in Christ (John 3:16)—a faith which will be expressed in love, hope and good works.

Likewise, the phrase *ecclesia reformata semper reformanda* ('the Church, having been reformed, is always in need of reformation') does not mean that the life of the Church needs to be in a state of perpetual revolution in which every aspect of faith and practice has to be continuously re-examined and thought out afresh. What it does mean is that visible churches are liable to error and that when they do err, they need to be reformed in line with biblical teaching (*reformanda secundum verbum Dei*, as the final words of the full version of the phrase put it).

Another Latin phrase which is often used and which needs careful unpacking is the *phrase lex orandi, lex credendi* ('the law of praying is the law of believing') and it is this phrase which will be the focus of this paper.

The origin of the phrase *lex orandi, lex credendi*

The phrase goes back to the work of the fifth-century theologian St Prosper of Aquitaine who wrote in the eighth chapter of a work entitled the *Indiculus Gratia Dei* ('Index Concerning the Grace of God'):

> Let us consider the sacraments of priestly prayers, which having been handed down by the apostles, are celebrated uniformly throughout the whole world and in every Catholic Church so that the law of praying might establish the law of believing (*ut legem credendi lex statuat supplicandi*).[2]

The *Indiculus* is a compilation of authoritative statements by the Popes on the subject of grace and it was written by St Prosper in his controversy with the semi-Pelagians, who held that God's grace was necessary neither for a person's first movement towards conversion nor for their final

---

[2] Text at Andre Marie, 'Lex Orandi Lex Credendi,' http://catholicism.org/lex-orandi-lex-credendi.html. '*Supplicandi*' here is the equivalent of '*orandi*.

perseverance in the faith. St Prosper disagreed and, following St Augustine, he argued for it being a matter of God's grace. He said that the prayers of the Catholic Church revealed her belief that salvation must be a work of God's initiative. He maintained that in the liturgy, the Church prays for the conversion of 'infidels', 'Jews" 'heretics,' 'schismatics' and 'the lapsed' because none of them would seek the true faith on their own.

As St Prosper puts it in the passage immediately following on from the sentence quoted above:

> For when the bishops of the holy peoples observe the mandates committed to them by office in the presence of divine mercy, they plead the cause of the human race, and while the whole Church sighs deeply with them, they entreat and pray that faith may be given to unbelievers, that idol worshippers may be freed from the errors of their impiety, that the light of truth may appear to the Jews, the veil over their heart having been removed, that heretics may regain their senses by perception of the Catholic faith, that schismatics may receive the spirit of revived charity, that the remedies of penance may be granted to the lapsed, and finally that the court of heavenly mercy may be opened to catechumens when they are led to the sacraments of regeneration. The effect of these very things demonstrates that they are not asked from the Lord either vainly or in a perfunctory manner: seeing that God deigns to draw many out of every kind of error, whom delivered from the power of darkness he might transfer into the kingdom of the Son of his charity (Col 1:13), and from vessels of wrath he might make vessels of mercy (Rom 9:22). This is so much thought to be entirely divine work, that to the God accomplishing these things

thanksgiving and praise are always rendered for the illumination or the correction of such people.[3]

Lex orandi, lex credendi in the Roman Catholic, Orthodox and Anglican traditions

St Prosper uses the idea that how the Church prays shows what the Church believes in a specific context. However, in the form of the phrase *lex orandi, lex credendi* his idea has become used as a general principle, the principle that how the Church prays helps to establish for us what the Church believes.

This principle is formally acknowledged in Roman Catholic theology. Thus, the *Catechism of the Catholic Church* declares:

> The Church's faith precedes the faith of the believer who is invited to adhere to it. When the Church celebrates the sacraments, she confesses the faith received from the apostles – whence the ancient saying: *lex orandi, lex credendi* (or: *legem credendi lex statuat supplicandi*, according to Prosper of Aquitaine [5th cent.]). The law of prayer is the law of faith: the Church believes as she prays.[4]

It is also an accepted part of Orthodox theology. Thus the Ecumenical Patriarch, Bartholomew I, declared in a homily to welcome Pope Benedict XVI to Constantinople in November 2006, 'we recognize that the rule of prayer is the rule of faith (*lex orandi, lex credendi*)' and used this principle as the basis for his argument that 'in liturgy, we are reminded of the need to reach unity in faith as well as in prayer.' 'The Liturgy teaches us,' he said, 'to broaden our horizon and vision, to speak the language of love

---

[3] *Indiculus* 8, translation by Daniel Van Slyke at
http://www.pcj.edu/journal/essays/vanslyke11-2.htm.
[4] *Catechism of the Catholic Church*, (London: Geoffrey Chapman, 1994, Paragraph 1124), p.258.

and communion, but also to learn that we must be with one another in spite of our differences and even divisions.'[5]

As well as being part of the Roman Catholic and Orthodox traditions, the belief in the principle *lex orandi, lex credendi* is also an important part of Anglicanism. One of the things that distinguishes Anglicanism from the Lutheran and Reformed traditions, which were also shaped by the Protestant Reformation in the 16th century, is that while in the latter theological authority has been given to a single confessional document such as the *Augsburg Confession* of 1530, the *Genevan Confession* of 1536, or the *Westminster Confession* of 1646, in Anglicanism theological authority has traditionally been given to a confessional document, the *Thirty-Nine Articles* of 1571 plus two liturgical documents, the 1662 *Book of Common Prayer* and the 1662 *Ordinal*.

This has meant that if you wanted to know, for example, what Anglicans believe about people's need for the saving grace of God, you would find the answer not only in Articles IX, X and XV of the *Thirty-Nine Articles*, but also in the confession of sin contained in the services of Morning and Evening Prayer in the *Book of Common Prayer* which runs as follows:

> Almighty and most merciful Father, We have erred, and strayed from thy ways like lost sheep, We have followed too much the devices and desires of our own hearts, We have offended against thy holy laws, We have left undone those things which we ought to have done, And we have done those things which we ought not to have done, And there is no health in us: But thou, O Lord, have mercy upon us miserable offenders; Spare thou them, O God, which confess their faults, Restore thou them that are penitent, According to thy promises declared unto

---

[5] Patriarch Bartholomew I, 'Homily by His All Holiness Patriarch Bartholomew during the Divine Liturgy on the Feast Day of St Andrew at the Patriarchal Cathedral of St George, November 30 2006' at https://andrew4jc.blogspot.com/2006/11/homily-by-his-all-holiness-ecumenical.html.

mankind in Christ Jesu our Lord: And grant, O most merciful Father, for his sake, That we may hereafter live a godly, righteous, and sober life, To the glory of thy holy Name. Amen.

Similarly, if you wanted to know what Anglicans believe about the ordained ministry you would find the answer not only in Articles XXIII, XXIV, XXVI, XXXII and XXXVI of the *Thirty-Nine Articles*, but also in the 1662 *Ordinal*. For example, the Articles are silent about what form the ordained ministry should take. It is in the *Ordinal* that we learn about the Anglican commitment to the historic threefold order of bishops, priests and deacons. In the words of the Preface to the *Ordinal*:

> It is evident unto all men diligently reading holy Scripture and ancient Authors, that from the Apostles' time there have been these Orders of Ministers in Christ's Church; Bishops, Priests, and Deacons. Which offices were evermore had in such reverend estimation, that no man might presume to execute any of them, except he were first called, tried, examined, and known to have such qualities as are requisite for the same; and also by publick Prayer, with Imposition of Hands, were approved and admitted thereunto by lawful authority. And therefore, to the intent that these Orders may be continued, and reverently used and esteemed, in the Church of England; No man shall be accounted or taken to be a lawful Bishop, Priest, or Deacon in the Church of England, or suffered to execute any of the said functions, except he be called, tried, examined, and admitted thereunto, according to the Form hereafter following, or hath had formerly Episcopal Consecration or Ordination.

This historic Anglican commitment to the doctrinal significance of the 1662 *Prayer Book* and the 1662 *Ordinal* remains in place today. In the Church of England, Canon A5 names the *Book of Common Prayer* and the *Ordinal* alongside the *Thirty-Nine Articles* as places where the Church of England's doctrine is to be found. Likewise, in Canon C15, the Declaration of Assent made by Church of England ministers declares that

6

in the *Book of Common Prayer* and the *Ordinal* together with the *Thirty-Nine Articles* the Church of England has 'borne witness to Christian truth' and those making the declaration affirm their loyalty to this 'inheritance of faith.' In the wider Anglican Communion, not all churches give the same level of doctrinal authority to the *Book of Common Prayer* and the *Ordinal* as the Church of England does. Nevertheless, across the Communion as a whole, 'The Thirty-Nine Articles, the Book of Common Prayer and the Ordinal [of] 1662 represent the historic sources of lawful doctrine for a church.'[6]

Furthermore, as new Prayer Books and Ordinals have been produced in the churches of the Anglican Communion during the 20th and 21st centuries, the principle of *lex orandi, lex credendi* has been extended to them as well. Thus, the constitution of the Anglican Church in Aotearoa, New Zealand and Polynesia states that it 'holds and maintains the Doctrine and Sacraments of Christ as the Lord has commanded in Holy Scripture' as explained not only in the three historic sources of Anglican doctrine, but also in 'A New Zealand Prayer Boo*k* – *He Karakia Mihinare o Aotearoa*.'[7]

The misunderstanding of *lex orandi, lex credendi* and the liturgical approach of the English Reformers

At the beginning of this paper, it was noted that the phrase *lex orandi, lex credendi* needs careful unpacking. This is because its meaning can be (and has been) misunderstood.

This misunderstanding arises when liturgy is seen as the basis for theology. We can see this misunderstanding, for instance, in the introduction to the 1985 *Book of Alternative Services* of the Anglican Church of Canada. This declares:

---

[6] *The Principles of Canon Law Common to the Churches of the Anglican Communion*, (London: Anglican Communion Office, 2008), p.58.
[7] Constitution of the Anglican Church in in Aotearoa, New Zealand and Polynesia, Part B.1.

It is precisely the intimate relationship of gospel, liturgy, and service that stands behind the theological principle lex orandi: lex credendi, i.e., the law of prayer is the law of belief. This principle, particularly treasured by Anglicans, means that theology as the statement of the Church's belief is drawn from the liturgy, i.e., from the point at which the gospel and the challenge of Christian life meet in prayer. The development of theology is not a legislative process which is imposed on liturgy; liturgy is a reflective process in which theology may be discovered. The Church must be open to liturgical change in order to maintain sensitivity to the impact of the gospel on the world and to permit the continuous development of a living theology.[8]

In this way of looking at the matter, which has been put forward by a number of theologians such as David Fagerberg,[9] Aidan Kavanagh[10] and Alexander Schmemann,[11] the law of prayer is the law of belief because it is the experience of worship that is, and should be, the basis for our theology. Christians meet together to worship God and theology develops as they reflect on this experience. This means that if we want to know what to believe, our liturgical experience is the place to go to find out.

From an orthodox Anglican point of view, however, it is not liturgical experience that comes first, but Scripture. It is Scripture rather than worship which is the primary source of our knowledge of God. In the classic words of Archbishop Thomas Cranmer:

> Unto a Christian man there can be nothing either more
> necessary or profitable, than the knowledge of Holy

---

[8] Anglican Church of Canada, *Book of Alternative Services*, (Toronto: Anglican Book Centre, 1985), p.10.

[9] David W. Fagerberg, *Theologia Prima: What is Liturgical Theology?*, (Chicago/Mundelein: Hillenbrand Books, 2004), pp.39–69.

[10] Aidan Kavanagh, *On Liturgical Theology*, (New York: Pueblo Publishing, 1984).

[11] Alexander Schmemann, *Liturgical Theology*, (Crestwood: St Vladimir's Seminary Press, 1990).

Scripture, forasmuch as in it is contained God's true word, setting forth his glory, and also man's duty. And there is no truth nor doctrine necessary for our justification and everlasting salvation, but that is (or may be) drawn out of that fountain and well of truth. Therefore as many as be desirous to enter into the right and perfect way unto God, must apply their minds to know Holy Scripture; without the which, they can neither sufficiently know God and his will, neither their office and duty.[12]

As he goes on to say:

Let us diligently search for the well of life in the books of the Old and New Testaments, and not run to the stinking puddles of men's traditions, devised by man's imagination, for our justification and salvation. For in Holy Scripture is fully contained what we ought to do, and what to eschew; what to believe, what to love, and what to look for at God's hands at length. In these books we shall find the Father from whom, the Son by whom, and the Holy Ghost, in whom all things have their being and keeping up, and these three persons to be but one God, and one substance. In these books we may learn to know ourselves, how vile and miserable we be, and also to know God, how good he is of himself, and how he maketh us and all creatures partakers of his goodness. We may learn also in these books to know God's will and pleasure, as much as (for this present time) is convenient for us to know.[13]

Because Cranmer and the other Reformers of the Church of England in the 16th and 17th centuries believed this they also believed that while

---

[12] Thomas Cranmer *A Fruitful Exhortation to the Reading and Knowledge of Holy Scripture* in John Leith (ed.) *Creeds of the Churches*, Oxford: Blackwell, 1973, p.231.
[13] Cranmer, *A Fruitful Exhortation*, p.232.

churches had the authority to establish their own liturgies this right was limited by what was in Scripture. As Article XX of the *Thirty-Nine Articles* puts it, they believed that: 'The Church hath power to decree rites or ceremonies, and authority in controversies of faith: and yet it is not lawful for the Church to ordain anything that is contrary to God's word written.'

The Anglican Reformers further believed that key parts of the practice of the medieval English church fell foul of this principle. For example, as Eamon Duffy explains in his book *The Stripping of the Altars,* praying for the dead in purgatory and the cult of the saints were key parts of English religion in the late medieval period. [14] However, the English Reformers rejected both as being contrary to Scripture. In the words of Article XXII, they held that: 'The Romish doctrine concerning Purgatory, Pardons, worshipping and adoration as well of Images as of Reliques, and also Invocation of Saints, is a fond thing vainly invented, and grounded upon no warranty of Scripture; but rather repugnant to the word of God.'

As result of this conviction, when Cranmer and his fellow Reformers began to develop a new liturgy for the Church of England during the reign of Edward VI, they gave no place to either praying for the dead, or continuing to invoke the saints, or adore their relics.

For the English Reformers, theology was seen as based on Scripture, rather than flowing from liturgical practice. Therefore, theology—and the liturgical practice resulting from it—required correction when they departed from what Scripture taught.

As well as seeking to correct the liturgical errors of the medieval Church in this way, the English Reformers also developed a positive alternative liturgical approach of their own which formed the basis for the *Book of Common Prayer* and the 1662 *Ordinal.* In developing this approach, their commitment to the normative role of Scripture in theology and in liturgy meant they developed a series of services in 'which nothing is ordained

---

[14] Eamon Duffy, *The Stripping of the Altars*, (New Haven and London: Yale UP, 1992).

to be read, but the very pure Word of God, the Holy Scriptures, or that which is agreeable to the same.'[15] What this conviction means in practice is that the services and other liturgical material contained in the *Book of Common Prayer* and the 1662 *Ordinal,* are largely made up of readings from Scripture, paraphrases of, and allusions to, Scripture, and summaries of biblical teaching. They are an attempt to express biblical theology in liturgical form.

It might be asked at this point what room this approach to liturgy leaves for the principle *lex orandi, lex credendi*. If the liturgy is simply a reflection of what is in the Bible then in what sense can liturgy in and of itself have authority for theology? The answer is that the liturgy (like other extra-biblical authorities such as the teaching of the Fathers, the Catholic Creeds and the confessions of faith produced at the Reformation) has authority precisely *because* it reflects what is in the Bible.

As Canon C15 suggests, the authority which the *Book of Common Prayer* and the 1662 *Ordinal* have is the authority of faithful witness. They rightly constitute a *lex credendi* because they faithfully point us to the teaching of the Bible and by so doing help shape our thinking and our behaviour, both in church and in our daily lives, so that they are increasingly in line with this teaching.

The principle that has governed the development of new forms of liturgy in the churches of the Anglican Communion is that 'Liturgical adaption and innovation must not be inconsistent with the Word of God and with the spirit and teaching of the Book of Common Prayer 1662.'[16] This has meant that, in theory at least, Anglican liturgy has continued to have proper authority because it has been in line with the teaching of Scripture.

It is also important to note that in insisting that the authority of liturgy rests on the prior authority of Scripture, this approach is in line with what

---

[15] *The Book of Common Prayer*, 'Concerning the Services of the Church,' 1662.
[16] *The Principles of Canon Law Common to the Churches of the Anglican Communion*, p.61.

St Prosper originally taught. As scholars such as Paul De Clerck[17] and Geoffrey Wainwright[18] have noted, St Prosper's argument in the *Indiculus* is based on the teaching of Paul in 1 Timothy 2:1–4 where the Apostle urges that 'supplications, prayers, intercessions, and thanksgivings be made for all men' because God 'desires all men to be saved and come to the knowledge of the truth.' In the words of Wainwright, St Prosper's argument is that:

> the apostolic injunction [1 Tim 2:1–4] to pray for the whole human race—which the church obeys in its intercessions—proves the obligation to believe with the holy see, that all faith, even the beginning of good will as well as growth and perseverance is from start to finish a work of grace.[19]

In other words, for St Prosper it is the teaching of the Bible, which the liturgical practice of the universal Church then reflects, that proves the point he wants to make about the priority of grace. Liturgical practice for him does not have a free-standing authority but is authoritative as a reflection of the teaching of Scripture. *Lex orandi* is *lex credendi* because it embodies the antecedent teaching of the Bible.

Three examples of the need for a right relationship between *lex orandi* and *lex credendi*

Three examples which highlight the need for a right relationship between what the Church does liturgically and what the Church believes theologically on the basis of Scripture are: the issue of the *filioque* clause, the issue of prayers for the dead and the story of the ordination of women in The Episcopal Church.

---

[17] Paul De Clerck, 'Lex Orandi, Lex Credendi': The Ordinal Sense and Historical Avatars of an Equivocal Adage,' *Studia Liturgica* 24, 1994, pp.178-200.
[18] Geoffrey Wainwright, *Doxology: The praise of God in Doctrine, Worship and Life*, (New York: OUP, 1990).
[19] Wainwright, *Doxology*, p.225.

a. The filioque clause

The Latin word *filioque* means 'and the son' and the '*filioque* clause' is the name that is given to the addition of the words 'and the son' to the original statement in the Nicene Creed that the Holy Spirit 'proceeds from the Father'. The historic and continuing disagreement between the Eastern and Western churches is whether it was and is legitimate to add these words to the original text of the Creed.

The original text of the Nicene Creed reflects the traditional belief of the Eastern Church that the Holy Spirit proceeds from the Father alone (known as the 'single procession' of the Spirit). From at least the fourth century onwards, however, Western theologians such as St Hilary of Poitiers taught that the Spirit proceeds from the Son as well as the Father (known as the 'double procession'). From the time of St Augustine onwards, belief in the double procession became accepted as the orthodox position in the Western Church and Western churches (including the Church of England) gradually came to use a version of the Nicene Creed with the *filioque* clause added as reflection of this belief.[20]

The versions of the Nicene Creed currently used by the Church of England in the *Book of Common Prayer* and *Common Worship* communion services both include the *filioque* clause. However, in the 1976 *Moscow Agreed Statement* of the Anglican-Orthodox Doctrinal Commission, the Anglican members recommended that the *filioque* clause should not be used.[21] This was also recommended by the Lambeth conferences of 1978 and 1988.[22]

---

[20] For details of the history of the addition of the *filioque* clause to the Creed, see John Kelly, *Early Christian Creeds*, 3rd Ed., (Harlow: Longman, 1972), pp.358-367.
[21] *Anglican Orthodox Dialogue, The Moscow Agreed Statement*, (London: SPCK, 1977), p.88.
[22] *Anglican Orthodox Dialogue*, p.88. Also, Roger Coleman (ed.), *Resolutions of the Twelve Lambeth Conferences 1867-1988*, (Toronto: Anglican Book Centre, 1992, pp.192), 201.

The reason given for Anglicans ceasing to use the clause was the lack of ecumenical agreement over belief in the double procession of the Holy Spirit. However, in response, it can be argued that theologically it is right to continue to use the clause because the Western belief in the double procession has the support of Scripture. In the words of Tom Smail:

> We need only recall such passages as John 15:26 which speaks of 'the Counsellor whom I send to you from the Father' and John 16:7, 'If I go I will send him to you,' and also the risen Jesus breathing upon his disciples and saying, 'Receive the Holy Spirit' (John 20:22). To such passages the West appeals for biblical backing and such an appeal is fully justified.[23]

What we declare in the liturgy needs to reflect biblical teaching. The Bible teaches that the Holy Spirit is the Spirit of Christ (Romans 8:29, Philippians 1:19, 1 Peter 1:11) who come us to us not only from the Father, but also from the Son. The river of life flows from 'the throne of God and the Lamb' (Revelation 22:1). It is not wrong for the East to declare that the Spirit proceeds from the Father (since this is biblical), but it is better to say with the West that he proceeds from the Father and the Son (since this reflects more of the biblical picture). Ecumenical agreement over liturgy is important, but expressing the fullness of biblical teaching through liturgy is more important still.

b. Prayers for the dead

As we noted above, the Anglican Reformers of the 16th century abandoned the traditional medieval practice of praying for the dead. In the Order for the Burial of the Dead in the *Book of Common Prayer,* there are no prayers offered for the dead. Instead '[t]he prayer in the Service is for ourselves, that we may come to "the unspeakable joys" of those who are in the immediate presence of their Lord.'[24]

---

[23] Tom Smail, *The Giving Gift,* (London: Hodder and Stoughton, 1988), p.132.
[24] W. H. Griffith Thomas, *The Catholic Faith,* (London: Church Book Room Press, 1960), p.185.

However, from the 17th century, individuals within the Church of England began to argue in favour of the propriety of praying for the dead. This position began to spread as a result of the impact of the Oxford Movement on the Church of England in the 19th century and the huge loss of life in the First World War. Since then, prayers for the dead have become widely used in the Church of England.

Nevertheless, those loyal to the teaching of the English Reformers have continued to resist the development and in 1971 the Archbishops' Commission on Christian Doctrine produced the report *Prayer and the Departed* which sought to bridge the gap between their position and the position of those who viewed prayers for the dead as legitimate.

This report set out the arguments for and against praying for the dead. It noted that those who support the practice hold that:

> Since it is entirely right and natural to express through prayer our thoughts and wishes and hopes for those on this earth whom we love within the family of God, why should these prayers cease the moment the person for whom they are offered passes through the thin veil which separates us from the more glorious life beyond? Prayer is a spontaneous expression of love, and since we love the departed, we cannot help praying for them.[25]

It also added that, in the view of those who hold this position, when we pray for the dead:

> we do not suggest that we are pleading with a reluctant God to change his mind or alter his purpose concerning them. Rather, we express a simple, trustful confidence in the loving care and mercy of a heavenly Father.[26]

[25] Archbishops' Commission on Christian Doctrine, *Prayer and the Departed*, (London: SPCK, 1971), p.19.
[26] *Prayer and the Departed*, p.19.

The report went on to explain that those opposed to the practice hold that:

> To pray for the Christian dead is unnecessary and doctrinally misleading: to pray for others who have died is improper. This life is the time for making an irrevocable choice either for God or against him. No change of direction is possible after death. If a person has been faithful on earth and has appropriated the benefits of the atonement, there is no need to pray that everlasting life and peace should come upon him. To pray that 'the faithful departed may rest in peace' is therefore doctrinally inconsistent, in that it implies that they are not at rest (else why should we pray for rest?) and that they do not have peace; and practically, it is pointless, since what is prayed for is already theirs. Alternatively, if a person has rejected God on earth, there will be no second chance hereafter. Those who pray for a second chance are thus attempting to pray a prayer in the name of Jesus which is not in accord with the will of God and are therefore doing something theologically improper.[27]

It added that they further believe that:

> Prayer should be based on promise. The only way we can approach our heavenly Father with confidence in prayer is along the paths he has shown us. Among the very many injunctions in Scripture to pray for the living there is not one to pray for the dead, and there is no sure example of prayers for the dead in the Bible. With neither promise, injunction, nor example to guide us, prayer for the dead would appear to have little warrant.[28]

In an attempt to find a way forward that both sides could accept, the Commission (which included the notable evangelicals Michael Green and

---

[27] *Prayer and the Departed*, p.22.
[28] *Prayer and the Departed*, p.24.

J I Packer) set out in the report five forms of prayer 'which could be used *ex animo* by Anglicans of all theological persuasions':[29]

The first four are for use when the person who has died has professed the Christian faith. They are:

'May God in his infinite love and mercy bring the whole Church, living and departed in the Lord Jesus, to a joyful resurrection and the fulfilment of his eternal kingdom.'

'We commend *N.* to God'

'We commend to God almighty this our brother *N.* here departed.'

'We thank thee, O God, for the life and witness of thy servant *N.*, whom we remember before you this day.' [30]

The fifth is a prayer for use when the person who has died was without explicit Christian faith:

> God of infinite mercy and justice, who hast made man in
> thine own image, and hatest nothing that thou hast made,
> we rejoice in thy love for all creation and commend all
> men to thee, that in them thy will be done, in and through
> Jesus Christ our Lord.[31]

Many evangelicals would still want to say that we should offer no prayers for the dead at all. However, in the case of these five prayers, it can be said that nothing in them contradicts the biblical witness and, positively, that what they ask for (namely, for God to bring his whole Church at the last into his eternal kingdom, and for God's will to be done in the lives of all people) is in line with biblical teaching.

---

[29] *Prayer and the Departed*, 51.
[30] *Prayer and the Departed*, pp.51-52.
[31] *Prayer and the Departed*, p.55.

The same cannot be said, however, for the prayers produced by the Church of England Liturgical Commission to resource the Church of England's commemoration of the First World War. These resources include a liturgy for a Eucharist of Remembrance including the following Collect, suggestion for areas of intercession and Post-Communion prayer:

> Lord of the nations, Saviour and judge of all: remove from human hearts all bitterness and hate, grant to those who have died in war your mercy and forgiveness and bring us all to the peace of your eternal Kingdom; through Jesus Christ our Lord, who suffered and died, and now lives and reigns with you and the Holy Spirit, one God, world without end. Amen.

> Pray for all those who mourn, for the establishing of a just peace and stability in the world, for victims of terror, those maimed and injured in war, the lost and forgotten, those whose names are not remembered, those haunted by dark memories and the depressed, the homeless and the broken-hearted; those who died violently and those who died as a result of injury, for those who went to the grave unable to tell their stories.

> Lord God, in this Eucharist which we have shared, you have spoken your word of life and nourished us with the mysteries of Christ's body and blood; bring us with all who have died in combat or through the injuries of war, to know the joys of heaven. We ask this through Jesus Christ, who lived and died and was raised to newness of life, to whom be glory in every age and for eternity. Amen.

> Give rest, O Christ, to your servants with your saints, where sorrow and pain are no more, neither sighing, but life everlasting.

All: And weeping o'er the grave we make our song: Alleluia, alleluia, alleluia.'[32]

As Andrew Goddard notes, in contrast with the prayers suggested in *Prayer and the Departed*, this material goes beyond the limits of biblical teaching. Rather than suggesting prayer for 'the whole Church, living and departing in the Lord Jesus', it suggests prayers for the salvation of all, whether Christian or non-Christian, who have died as a result of war. By so doing, it implies that salvation may be available apart from a relationship with Christ and even feeds the idea that people may be saved *because* they have died in war.[33]

As Goddard goes on to ask:

> How can such prayers be faithful to justification by grace through faith in Christ alone and the reality that 'Just as people are destined to die once, and after that to face judgment, so Christ was sacrificed once to take away the sins of many; and he will appear a second time, not to bear sin, but to bring salvation to those who are waiting for him' (Hebrews 9:27–28)?

As we have seen, when properly understood, the principle of *lex orandi, lex credendi* entails that what the Church prays should be in line with the teaching of Scripture. This is true of the model prayers in *Prayer and the Departed*, but it is not true of the prayers for remembrance from the Liturgical Commission.

c.   *The ordination of women in the Episcopal Church*

The two examples we have just looked at illustrate the point that Scripture is the basis on which we have to assess the Church's officially agreed

---

[32] Propers for a Eucharist of Remembrance at https://www.churchofengland.org/prayer-and-worship/worship-texts-and-resources/church-england-world-war-one/propers-eucharist-remembrance.
[33] Andrew Goddard, 'Can we pray for the dead?' at https://www.fulcrum-anglican.org.uk/articles/can-we-pray-for-the-dead/.

liturgical practice. The example we are now going to look at—the story of the ordination of women in the Episcopal Church in the United States—illustrates the further point that Scripture is also the basis on which we have to assess liturgical actions which contravene the Church's officially agreed practice.

In the Episcopal Church, as in other provinces of the Anglican Communion, the 20th century saw both growing pressure for the ordination of women and continuing opposition to this development. What was distinctive about what took place in the Episcopal Church is that, unlike in other provinces, the first ordination of women to the diaconate and the priesthood took place when this was still contrary to the church's agreed teaching.

Like the Church of England, the Episcopal Church admitted women to the order of deaconesses by means of the laying on of hands from the second half of the 19th century. However, it did not permit women to become deacons, priests or bishops.

In 1965, however, Bishop James Pike of California ordained Phyliss Edwards as a deacon. Although this action was not recognised by the Episcopal Church at the time, in 1970, the Episcopal Church decided to ordain women as deacons. The first officially agreed ordinations of women deacons then took place in 1971.

In 1973, the Episcopal Church's General Convention rejected the ordination of women to the priesthood—but, in 1974, eleven deacons were ordained as priests by two retired and one resigned episcopal bishop at a service at Philadelphia. Like the ordination of Phyliss Edwards, these ordinations were not recognised by the Episcopal Church—but, two years later, General Convention agreed that women might be ordained as both priests and bishops. The first official ordination of women priests then took place in 1977 and Barbara Harris was consecrated as Suffragan Bishop of Massachusetts in 1989.

The question raised by this history is whether it is legitimate to perform liturgical actions (in this case ordination) which are against what a particular church currently teaches. The answer to this question is that, in principle, it might be right to do so.

Imagine, for example, a church whose teaching forbad people of different races receiving Holy Communion together. It would generally be accepted that it would be right to ignore such teaching and to allow people of whatever race to receive Holy Communion together as the Christian Church as a whole has done since earliest times. The reason for this is that sharing Holy Communion together manifests the unity that all Christians possess, as members of the one body of Christ, a unity that transcends all racial divisions (Romans 12:5 1 Corinthians 10:17, Galatians 3:28). Conversely, refusing to share Holy Communion with someone of a different race would involve refusing to acknowledge the trans-racial unity Christ died to achieve (Ephesians 2:11–22).

What this example highlights, once again, is that we need to give Holy Scripture the last word on the matter. To go back to the story of the ordination of women in the Episcopal Church, the only way we can rightly decide whether the ordinations that took place in 1965 and 1974 were brave acts of prophetic witness, or unjustified rejections of church order, is by deciding whether it is right in principle for women to be ordained as deacons or priests—and this is something that we can only decide by looking at what the New Testament tells us about the role of women in the Church and its ministry.

Thus, if the teaching of passages such as 1 Corinthians 14:34–36 or 1 Timothy 2:11–15 means that women should never exercise leadership or teaching roles in church, then their ordination would be wrong and so it was wrong for women to be ordained in 1965 and 1974. Conversely, if passages such as Romans 16:1–7 and 1 Timothy 3:11 indicate that women did exercise ministerial roles in the Apostolic Church, then it can be argued that the ordinations in 1965 and 1974 were right in principle, even if it might have been better to await the official agreement of the Episcopal

Church and the wider Anglican Communion rather than pre-empting it.[34]

The three examples considered in this section underline the point that, to be legitimate, what takes place liturgically has be able to be in line with biblical teaching rather than go against it. *Lex orandi* needs to be in accordance with *lex credendi* and both need to be in accordance with Scripture. With this in mind, we shall now go on to look at the current proposals for the Church of England to give liturgical affirmation to same-sex relationships and gender transition.

Proposals for the liturgical affirmation of same-sex relationships in the Church of England

The 2013 *Report of the House of Bishops Working Group on Human Sexuality* (the 'Pilling' Report) had as one of its 'findings and recommendations' that 'there can be circumstances where a priest, with the agreement of the relevant PCC, should be free to mark the formation of permanent same-sex relationship in a public service.'[35]

The House of Bishops' shared conversations of human sexuality have now come to an end and its new teaching document on marriage and sexuality is being drawn up. One of the ideas that is being floated as a way forward for the Church of England is the implementation of this recommendation by allowing services of 'blessing' or 'welcome' for same-sex couples who are in Civil Partnership or same-sex civil 'marriage.'

---

[34] For the arguments on how to interpret the Bible on this issue see John Piper and Wayne Grudem (eds),
Recovering Biblical Manhood and Womanhood, (Wheaton: Crossway Books, 2012) and Ronald W Pierce and
Rebecca Merrill Groothuis (eds), *Discovering Biblical Equality,* (Leicester: Apollos, 2005).
[35] *Report of the House of Bishops Working Group on human sexuality,* (London: Church House Publishing, 2013), p.151.

For example, in an article entitled 'Battle looms in Church of England over "blessings" for gay marriage' published in *Christian Today* on 4 July 2016, Ruth Gledhill writes:

> There is unlikely to be any attempt to change the definition of marriage. However, progressives are hoping for a move towards allowing church services of recognition for civil partnerships and same-sex marriages. Calling such services 'blessings' would be problematic, but they could be given another name such as 'services of welcome'.[36]

There are two forms which the implementation of the Pilling recommendation might take. One would involve the provision of an agreed form of liturgy for clergy who wish to use it and the other would simply give permission to individuals and groups to develop their own liturgies for this purpose. However, what both have in common is that they would mean that the Church of England would be happy for its clergy to offer a public liturgical affirmation of same-sex relationships (including same-sex 'marriages').

A specific proposal has now been put forward by the Diocesan Synod of the Diocese of Hereford which passed a motion on 19 October 2017 stating:

> That this Synod request the House of Bishops to commend an Order of Prayer and Dedication after the registration of a civil partnership or a same-sex marriage for use by ministers in exercise of their discretion under Canon B4, being a form of service neither contrary to, nor indicative of any departure from, the doctrine of the Church of England in any essential matter, together with

---

[36] Text at:
http://www.christiantoday.com/article/battle.looms.in.church.of.england.over.blessings.for.gay.marriage/89832.htm .

guidance that no parish should be obliged to host, nor minister conduct, such a service.[37]

A Private Members Motion on similar lines in the name of Christina Baron of the Diocese of Bath and Wells is also currently gathering signatures among the members of General Synod.[38]

If the service called for in these motions followed the pattern of the existing service of 'Prayer and Dedication after a Civil Marriage', it would involve a same-sex couple dedicating their marriage to God and being blessed and prayed for as they embark on their new life together.[39]

Why these proposals go against the principle of *lex orandi, lex credendi*

Both the general proposal for the blessing of same-sex relationships by the Church of England and the specific proposal contain in the Hereford motion would violate the principle of *lex orandi, lex credendi.*

To understand why this is the case, the key point to grasp is that any decision to allow the liturgical affirmation of same-sex relationships has to be based on the belief that God approves of such action and therefore of the relationship which is being affirmed. Otherwise, the Church of England's action will be completely apostate and in total disregard of what God thinks about the matter. As J I Packer rightly notes:

[37] David Pocklington, "CofE Service After Same Sex Marriage?" in *Law & Religion UK*, 20 October 2017,
http://www.lawandreligionuk.com/2017/10/20/cofe-service-after-same-sex-marriage/.
[38] 'Liturgies for same sex couples' at
https://www.churchofengland.org/more/policy-and-thinking/work-general-synod/diocesan-synod-motions#na.
[39] See 'An Order for Prayer and Dedication after a Civil Marriage' in *Common Worship: Pastoral Services*,
(London: Church House Publishing, 2000), pp.173-183.

To bless same-sex unions liturgically is to ask God to bless them and to enrich those who join in them, as is done in marriage ceremonies. This assumes that the relationship, of which the physical bond is an integral part, is intrinsically good and thus, if I may coin a word, blessable, as procreative sexual intercourse within heterosexual marriage is.[40]

For the Church of England to declare through its liturgical actions that this is the case would be to violate a series of statements about marriage and human sexuality to which it is already officially committed.

The *Book of Common Prayer* marriage service depicts marriage as taking place between a man and a woman. Thus, it says that at a wedding those who are gathered together have done so 'to join together this man and this woman in holy matrimony.'

Canon B30 declares that:

The Church of England affirms, according to our Lord's teaching, that marriage is in its nature a union permanent and lifelong, for better for worse, till death them do part, of one man with one woman, to the exclusion of all others on either side, for the procreation and nurture of children, for the hallowing and right direction of the natural instincts and affections, and for the mutual society, help and comfort which the one ought to have of the other, both in prosperity and adversity.[41]

The motion passed by General Synod in November 1987 states:

This Synod affirms that the biblical and traditional teaching on chastity and fidelity in personal relationships

---

[40] J I Packer, 'Why I Walked,' *Banner of Truth*, January 27, 2003, at https://banneroftruth.org/uk/resources/articles/2003/why-i-walked/.
[41] *The Canons of the Church of England*, 5ed, (London: Church House Publishing, 1993), p.49.

is a response to, and expression of, God's love for each one of us, and in particular affirms:

- that sexual intercourse is an act of total commitment which belongs properly within a permanent married relationship;
- that fornication and adultery are sins against this ideal, and are to be met by a call to repentance and the exercise of compassion;
- that homosexual genital acts also fall short of this ideal, and are likewise to be met with a call to repentance and the exercise of compassion;
- that all Christians are called to be exemplary in all spheres of morality, and that holiness of life is particularly required of Christian leaders.'[42]

The 1991 House of Bishops report *Issues in Human Sexuality* argues that what it calls a 'homophile' orientation and attraction could not be endorsed by the Church as:

> a parallel and alternative form of human sexuality as complete within the terms of the created order as the heterosexual. The convergence of Scripture, Tradition and reasoned reflection on experience, even including the newly sympathetic and perceptive thinking of our own day, make it impossible for the Church to come with integrity to any other conclusion.
>
> Heterosexuality and homosexuality are not equally congruous with the observed order of creation or with the insights of revelation as the Church engages with these in the light of her pastoral ministry.'[43]

---

[42] *General Synod Report of Proceedings,* Vol 18 No 3, (London: Church House Publishing, 1987), pp.955-956.
[43] *Issues in Human Sexuality,* (London: Church House Publishing, 1991), p.40.

Resolution 1.10 of the 1998 Lambeth Conference declares that the Conference:

> in view of the teaching of Scripture, upholds faithfulness in marriage between a man and a woman in lifelong union, and believes that abstinence is right for those who are not called to marriage.'

It also declares that the Conference 'cannot advise the legitimising or blessing of same-sex unions nor ordaining those involved in same gender unions.'[44]

The 1999 House of Bishops teaching document *Marriage* states that:

> Marriage is a pattern that God has given in creation, deeply rooted in our social instincts, through which a man and a woman may learn love together over the course of their lives ... Sexual intercourse, as an expression of faithful intimacy, belongs within marriage exclusively.'[45]

The Preface to the *Common Worship* marriage service tells the congregation that:

> Marriage is a gift of God in creation through which husband and wife may know the grace of God. It is given that as man and woman grow together in love and trust, they shall be united with one another in heart, body and mind, as Christ is united with his bride, the Church.[46]

---

[44] *The Official Report of the Lambeth Conference 1998*, (Harrisburg: Morehouse Publishing, 1999), p.381.
[45] House of Bishops, *Marriage*, (London: Church House Publishing, 1999), pp.7-8.
[46] Text at https://www.churchofengland.org/prayer-worship/worship/texts/pastoral/marriage/marriage.aspx.

The 2005 *House of Bishops Pastoral Statement on Civil Partnerships* states:

> It has always been the position of the Church of England that marriage is a creation ordinance, a gift of God in creation and a means of his grace. Marriage, defined as a faithful, committed, permanent and legally sanctioned relationship between a man and a woman, is central to the stability and health of human society. It continues to provide the best context for the raising of children.

> The Church of England's teaching is classically summarised in *The Book of Common Prayer*, where the marriage service lists the causes for which marriage was ordained, namely: 'for the procreation of children ... for a remedy against sin [and] ... for the mutual society, help, and comfort that the one ought to have of the other.'

> In the light of this understanding the Church of England teaches that 'sexual intercourse, as an expression of faithful intimacy, properly belongs within marriage exclusively' (*Marriage: a teaching document of the House of Bishops*, 1999). Sexual relationships outside marriage, whether heterosexual or between people of the same sex, are regarded as falling short of God's purposes for human beings.' [47]

The statement goes on to say:

> It is likely that some who register civil partnerships will seek some recognition of their new situation and pastoral support by asking members of the clergy to provide a blessing for them in the context of an act of worship. The

---

[47] House of Bishops Pastoral Statement on Civil Partnerships, paragraphs 2-4, text at https://www.churchofengland.org/sites/default/files/2017-11/House%20of%20Bishops%20Statement%20on%20Civil%20Partnerships%202005.pdf.

House believes that the practice of the Church of England needs to reflect the pastoral letter from the Primates of the Anglican Communion in Pentecost 2003 which said:

'The question of public rites for the blessing of same-sex unions is still a cause of potentially divisive controversy. The Archbishop of Canterbury spoke for us all when he said that it is through liturgy that we express what we believe, and that there is no theological consensus about same-sex unions. Therefore, we as a body cannot support the authorisation of such rites'.

One consequence of the ambiguity contained within the new legislation is that people in a variety of relationships will be eligible to register as civil partners, some living consistently with the teaching of the Church, others not. In these circumstances it would not be right to produce an authorised public liturgy in connection with the registering of civil partnerships. In addition, the House of Bishops affirms that clergy of the Church of England should not provide services of blessing for those who register a civil partnership.[48]

Finally, the House of Bishops *Pastoral Guidance on Same-sex Marriage* stated that the same principles should apply with same-sex 'marriages' as with civil partnerships and that, in consequence, 'Services of blessing should not be provided. Clergy should respond pastorally and sensitively in other ways.'[49]

In the light of these declarations the only way that the Church of England could permit with integrity services of affirmation for same-sex partnerships including 'marriages' (which would in reality be services of

---

[48] House of Bishops Pastoral Statement, paragraphs, 16-17.
[49] House of Bishops Pastoral Guidance on Same-sex Marriages, paragraph 21, text at https://www.churchofengland.org/more/media-centre/news/house-bishops-pastoral-guidance-same-sex-marriage.

blessing, even if they were called something else) would be to repudiate all the statements just listed and declare that it now believes something else instead. Only in this way could the principle of *lex orandi, lex credendi*—that the Church of England prays as it believes—be maintained.

However, as we have also seen, in Anglican theology (as in the work of St Prosper of Aquitaine), what the Church believes is based on the teaching of Scripture. So, to move rightly to a new theological position, the Church of England would need to be able to show that affirming same-sex relationships as marriages (or partnerships equivalent to marriage) is in line with biblical teaching.

This cannot be done. In Scripture, marriage is established by God at creation as a life-long, exclusive, sexual union between one man and one woman—in principle, open to procreation (Genesis 2:24, Matthew 19:3–6). All forms of sexual activity outside of marriage thus defined are seen explicitly or implicitly as what the New Testament calls *porneia*—forms of sexual sin which have no place in the life of God's people. This includes all forms of same-sex sexual activity (see Genesis 19, Judges 19:22–30, Leviticus 18:22, 20:13, Deuteronomy 23:17–18, Mark 7:21, Acts 15:29, Romans 1:26–27, 1 Corinthians 6:9–1, 1 Timothy 1:10, Jude 7).[50]

No provision is made in Scripture for same-sex 'marriages' or partnerships and there is no theological room within the teaching of Scripture for them to exist. As Michael Brown observes:

- Every single reference to marriage in the entire Bible speaks of heterosexual unions without exception, to the point that a Hebrew idiom for marriage is for a man 'to take a wife'.

---

[50] See Richard Hays, *The Moral Vision of the New Testament*, (Edinburgh: T&T Clark, 1995), Ch.16; Robert Gagnon, *The Bible and Homosexual Practice*, (Nashville Abingdon, 2001); Michael Brown, *Can You Be Gay and Christian?*, (Lake Mary: Front Line, 2014); Martin Davie, *Studies on the Bible and Same-Sex Relationships since 2003*, (Malton: Gilead, 2015).

- Every warning to men about sexual purity presupposes heterosexuality, with the married man often warned not to lust after another woman.
- Every discussion about family order and structure speaks explicitly in heterosexual terms, referring to husbands and wives, fathers and mothers.
- Every law or instruction given to children presupposes heterosexuality, as children are urged to heed or obey or follow the counsel or example of their father and mother.
- Every parable, illustration or metaphor having to do with marriage is presented in exclusively heterosexual terms.

In the Old Testament, God depicts his relationship with Israel as that of a groom and a bride; in the New Testament, the image shifts to the marital union of husband and wife as a picture of Christ and the Church.[51]

It is because Scripture is thus clear about the matter that not only the Church of England but also the entire Christian tradition in all its forms has consistently upheld a pattern of sexual ethics based on either heterosexual marriage or sexual abstinence and has rejected same-sex sexual relationships as intrinsically sinful.[52]

This being the case, there is no place within the principle of *lex orandi, lex credendi* as Anglicans have understood it for the Church of England to allow for the liturgical affirmation of same-sex partnerships. The marriage service in the *Book of Common Prayer* declares 'that so many as are coupled together otherwise than God's Word doth allow are not joined together by God; neither is their Matrimony lawful' ('lawful' not just according to the law of the state, but according to the law of God).

All forms of same-sex sexual partnerships (same-sex marriages included) are examples of relationships 'otherwise than God's Word doth allow.' It is for this reason that the Church of England as a church, with a liturgy

---

[51] For this point see Brown, *Can You Be Gay and Christian?*, pp.86-90.
[52] See S, Donald Fortson and Rollin G. Grams, *Unchanging Witness*, (Nashville: B&H Academic, 2016).

based on Scripture, cannot give any form of liturgical affirmation to such relationships.

The proposal for affirming gender transition

In July 2017, General Synod endorsed a motion from the Diocese of Blackburn which declared 'that this Synod, recognising the need for transgender people to be welcomed and affirmed in their parish church, call on the House of Bishops to consider whether some nationally commended liturgical materials might be prepared to mark a person's gender transition.'[53]

Gender transition is the process by which someone who has male biology and who has previously been identified as male comes to identify themselves by what they see as their true female identity and *vice versa*. If they are Christians, they may well want to have this new identity publicly marked by the Church before God and his people, and the motion passed by Synod called for the bishops to consider whether new liturgical materials should be developed for this purpose.

The response from the House of Bishops, published as GS Misc 1178 *An Update on 'Welcoming Transgender People'*, [54] was not to agree to authorise new material, but to suggest that gender transition may appropriately be marked using the existing services of Baptism, Confirmation and the Affirmation of Baptismal Faith. As paragraph 4 of the bishops' response puts it:

> After taking time to consider the issue prayerfully, the House would like to encourage ministers to respond to any such requests in a creative and sensitive way. If not already received, baptism and confirmation are the

---

[53] 'Welcoming Transgender People' at
https://www.churchofengland.org/more/media-centre/news/welcoming-transgender-people.
[54] House of Bishops, GS Misc 1178 *An Update on 'Welcoming Transgender People'*, 2017, *para.4.*

normative ways of marking a new or growing faith in Jesus Christ. If the enquirer is already baptized and confirmed, the House notes that the Affirmation of Baptismal Faith, found in Common Worship, is an ideal liturgical rite which trans people can use to mark this moment of personal renewal.

It is not entirely clear what the bishops are saying about how the rites of Baptism, Confirmation and the Affirmation of Baptismal Faith should be used to mark someone's gender transition. Paragraph 8 of their response promises guidance later in the year. However, on the basis of existing unofficial services created to mark gender transition, it seems likely that what would be involved would be people who had undergone gender transition being baptised or confirmed or re-affirming their baptism in their assumed identity, using a name and pronouns consistent with that identity. Thus, if Mark became Carol in a male to female transition then Carol would be the name that would be used, and so would female pronouns and terms such as 'daughter' rather than 'son.'

Why this proposal is also problematic

This proposal by the bishops, if agreed, would mark a new *lex orandi* in the Church of England. Henceforth, the Church of England would be declaring through its authorised liturgical actions that it was an acceptable part of Christian discipleship for someone with male biology to identify themselves as female and *vice versa*.[55]

---

[55] It is important to distinguish such people from the tiny number of human beings (around 0.018% of live births) who suffer from a developmental disorder stemming from the Fall that means that they either have elements of both male and female in their biology or have a body whose observable physical characteristics cannot be classified as either male or female. Such 'intersex' individuals have to find a path of Christian discipleship that honours God's creation of human beings as male and female in the context of their own ambiguous physical condition. This is a different situation from someone who is indisputably either male or female in their biological make up.

This would not violate the principle *lex orandi, lex credendi* by going against any specific existing teaching of the Church of England. The Church of England currently has no specific teaching on this matter. The nearest we get to this is a 2003 memo from the House of Bishops which simply records that at that time different bishops thought that there were two views which could properly be held:

> The House recognised that there was a range of views within the Church on transsexualism and accepted that (as matters stood at present) both the positions set out below could properly be held: a) some Christians concluded on the basis of Scripture and Christian anthropology, that concepts such as 'gender reassignment' or 'sex change' were really a fiction. Hormone treatment or surgery might change physical appearance, but they could not change the fundamental God-given reality of 'male and female He created them' b) others, by contrast, whilst recognising that medical opinion was not unanimous, were persuaded that there were individuals whose conviction that they were 'trapped in the wrong body' was so profound and persistent that medical intervention, which might include psychiatric, hormone, and surgical elements, was legitimate and that the result could properly be termed a change of sex or gender.[56]

What the bishops' proposal would violate, however, is the point noted above that liturgical developments can only have legitimacy if they are in line with the teaching of Scripture. A *lex orandi* that goes against the teaching of Scripture is automatically illegitimate.

Scripture, reason and the Christian tradition teach us that, in his goodness and wisdom, God made human beings as a unity of body and soul. Rocks are purely material, angels are purely spiritual, but human

---

[56] Text at HB (03)M1 – House of Bishops: Summary of Decisions from the meeting of the House held 13-16 January 2003.

beings are a unity of a material body and an immaterial soul. This unity means that we are our bodies and our bodies are us, which is why it makes sense to say I got up in the morning, I ate and drank, and I went to bed at night. All these are actions of the single self who is both body and soul.

It is as this unity of body and soul that we are either male or female. To be male or female is to have certain bodily characteristics that are designed to enable us to fulfil God's command to 'be fruitful and multiply' (Genesis 1:28) by playing a particular role in the procreation and nurture of children.

Although death leads to a separation of the body and the soul, so fundamental are our bodies to who we are that God will resurrect our bodies at the end of time, just as he resurrected the body of Jesus. We will exist for all eternity as the male and female human beings God created us to be (see 1 Corinthians 15).

All this being the case, it is not right for people with male or female bodies to claim either that they are really a member of the other sex, or that that they have some other kind of sexual identity. This claim involves a rejection of our responsibility to acknowledge and accept with gratitude the truth about who God has made us to be as manifested to us in the nature of our bodies. As Oliver O'Donovan puts it:

> The sex into which we have been born (assuming it is physiologically unambiguous) is given to us to be welcomed as the gift of God. The task of psychological maturity – for it is a moral task, and not merely an event which may or may not transpire – involves accepting this gift and learning to love it, even though we may have to acknowledge that it does not come to us without problems. Our task is to discern the possibilities for personal relationship which are given to us with this biological sex, and to seek to develop them in accordance with our individual vocations. Those for whom this task has been comparatively unproblematic (though I suppose that no human being alive has been without some sexual

problems) are in no position to pronounce any judgement on those for whom accepting their sex has been so difficult that they have fled from it into denial. Nevertheless, we cannot and must not conceive of physical sexuality as a mere raw material with which we can construct a form of psychosexual self-expression which is determined only by the free impulse of our spirits. Responsibility in sexual development implies a responsibility to nature – to the ordered good of the bodily form which we have been given.[57]

What this means is that while we should have enormous compassion for those who suffer from what is known as gender dysphoria and who therefore feel that they cannot identify with the sex of their body, we cannot for this reason affirm the alternative identities to which they aspire. This is not who God has made them to be and, therefore, it is not who they truly are. It is not legitimate for us, or for them, to reject how God has made them.

Furthermore, it is not right either to affirm people's desire to live as members of the opposite sex, because this involves violating the biblical teaching that we should live as the members of the sex that God has given to us. This teaching can be found in Deuteronomy 22:5 which prohibits cross-dressing on the grounds that 'to dress after the manner of the opposite sex was to infringe the normal order of creation which divided humanity into male and female'.[58] It can also be found in 1 Corinthians 11:2–16 where Paul tells the Corinthians that men should follow the dress and hair codes which proclaim them to be male and women the codes which proclaim them to be female because 'God's creation needs humans to be fully, gloriously and truly human, which means fully and truly male

---

[57] Oliver O'Donovan, *Begotten or Made?*, (Oxford: OUP, 1984, pp.28-29).
[58] P.J. Harland 'Menswear and Womenswear: A Study of Deuteronomy 22:5,' *Expository Times*, 110, No.3, 1988, p.76.

and female.'[59] This does not mean that people should uncritically embrace the gender stereotypes of any given society. What it does mean is that they should live in a way that proclaims to that society the truth of God's creation of human beings as male and female.

It is now often said that is necessary to affirm people's desire to identify with, and live as, a member of their desired sex because this is the way that they will achieve psychological wellbeing. As noted above, it is for this reason that some members of the House of Bishops supported gender transition back in 2003. This argument was also to the fore in the General Synod debate on the Blackburn motion.

However, the claim that transitioning to live as a member of their desired sex is the best way forward for people with gender dysphoria is called into question by the available evidence, which fails to demonstrate that transition is successful in resolving the mental and physical health issues experienced by transgender people.[60] Scepticism about gender transition is expressed both by well qualified experts in the field of mental health and by a growing number of people who are explaining the reasons why, having gone through gender transition, they then decided to revert back to living in their birth sex.[61]

---

[59] Tom Wright, *Paul for Everyone - 1 Corinthians*, (London: SPCK, 2003, p.143).
[60] For example, a major Swedish study published in 2011 looking at the long term outcomes for people who had undergone sex-reassignment surgery found 'substantially higher rates of overall mortality, death from cardiovascular disease and suicide, suicide attempts, and psychiatric hospitalisations in sex-reassigned transsexual individuals compared to a healthy control population.' (Cecilia Djehne et al, 'Long-Term Follow-Up of Transsexual Persons Undergoing Sex Reassignment Surgery: Cohort Study in Sweden,' *PLoS One*, 6 (No.2), 2011).
[61] See for example, Paul McHugh. 'Transgenderism: A Pathogenic Meme', *Public Discourse*, 10 June 2015 at http://www.thepublicdiscourse.com/2015/06/15145/. See also Walt Heyer, *A Transgender's Faith*, Walt Heyer, 2015 and the testimonies in the 2017 documentary film *Tranzformed* (https://tranzformed.org/).

Rather than affirming that it is right for transgender people to reject their God-given sex, what Christians need to do instead is truly to love transgender people as the men and women God created them to be. Such love means a long-term commitment to giving them the spiritual, emotional and psychiatric support necessary to help them find healing and wholeness by accepting who they truly are and living accordingly. What the bishops propose in GS Mic 1178 would not be an expression of this kind of love and, for that reason, their proposal should be rejected.

Conclusion

When rightly understood, the principle *lex orandi, lex credendi* provides a useful tool for assessing both a church's liturgy and its doctrine. A church's liturgical practice needs to cohere with its doctrine and both need to be in line with Scripture. As we have seen in this paper, the use of this tool shows us that not only are proposals for marking same-sex relationships unacceptable, but so also is the new proposal to use liturgy to mark gender transition.

The teaching of the Bible and the historic teaching of the Christian tradition about human sexuality is all of a piece. They tell us that God created human beings as male and female, with men and women each having their own distinctive biology oriented in different ways to the procreation and nurture of children. They also tell us that God created marriage as a union between one man and one woman and that this forms the proper God given context for sexual intercourse and for fulfilling the divine command to 'be fruitful and multiply' (Genesis 1:28). It is for this reason that it would not be right for the Church of England to affirm liturgically either same-sex relationships or gender transition. Orthodox Anglicans therefore need to say an unequivocal 'no' to both proposals.

If you have enjoyed this book, you might like to consider:

- supporting the work of the Latimer Trust
- reading more of our publications
- recommending them to others

See www.latimertrust.org for more information.

Anglican Foundations by Tim Patrick

This handbook offers an introduction to the full suite of doctrinally determinative documents of the English Reformation. It supplies an orientation to each family of documents, as well as to the individual texts that were sanctioned by the church, state and crown. In addition to descriptions of the texts, there is also a brief history of each type of formulary, discussions of their varied purposes, and lists of key references for further reading.

The Anglican Church can only benefit from a fuller understanding of its own documentary heritage. Anglican Foundations is an unparalleled resource that offers students, ordinands, and all committed Anglicans the ideal orientation to the doctrinal texts of the English Reformation.

"This book is an essential resource for anyone with a serious interest in Anglicanism, both past and present."

Rev. Prof. Gerald Bray

Transgender Liturgies

In April 2015 Blackburn Diocesan Synod passed the following motion: 'That this Synod, recognising the need for transgender people to be welcomed and affirmed in their parish church, calls on the House of Bishops to consider whether some nationally commended liturgical materials might be prepared to mark a person's gender transition'.

The purpose of this study is to consider whether it would be right for the members of General Synod to vote in favour of this motion. It explains in more detail what the motion proposes and the theological implications and analyses the arguments for and against this motion. Ultimately, it explains why this means it would not be right to support the Blackburn motion.

Thinking Aloud

Christians today are faced with pressure to change and accommodate, both from outside and from within the church community. Nowhere does this seem to be more true than on the issue of human sexuality.

This volume discusses the issue with particular interest in the impact of recent events and publications on the Church of England.

Its collection of papers and reviews aims to spell out the biblical foundations for Christian thinking about sexuality and to offer an incisive critique which can inform our response to this pressure.

Lightning Source UK Ltd.
Milton Keynes UK
UKHW041116120219
337017UK00001B/9/P